NORTH
NORFOLK
COAST

THE coast of North Norfolk has always been dominated by the North Sea. For centuries man has earned his living from it, tried to control it by building sea defences, even to scorn it with flimsy piers, and always forfeited lives to it. The sea's influence may not appear so great today; few men now are dependent on it for their living, people are more comfortable and the defences are stronger. But there are always reminders of the North Sea's unpredictable power, from the haunting monument to lost lifeboat men of Wells (left), to the sight of the sea crashing over Cromer's sea wall as a gale strikes the coast, (opposite).

Many people will remember the North Norfolk coast for its wild seas and dramatic skies, but it is an area of many moods and for the past few years the photographer, Alan Blair, has sought to record this ever changing landscape on film. The result is this beautiful collection of photographs covering the coast from Wells-next-the-Sea to Happisburgh, the first in a new series of books on East Anglia.

The harbour at Wells-next-the-Sea

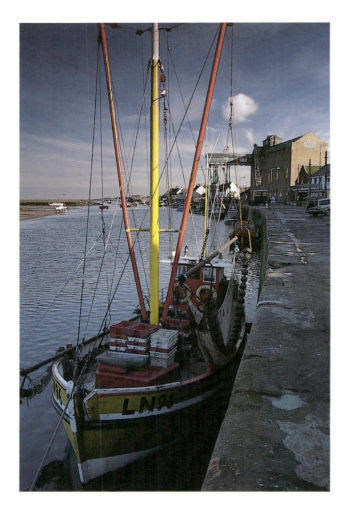

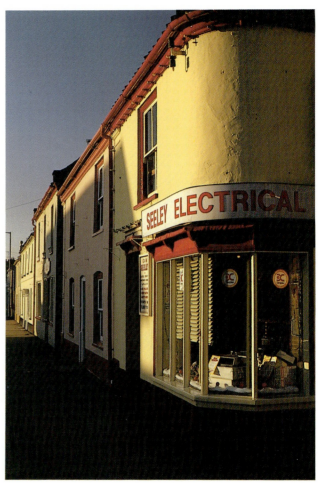

Wells quay and Freeman Street

Wells beach

Stiffkey church and the Old Hall

Autumn evening at Blakeney quay

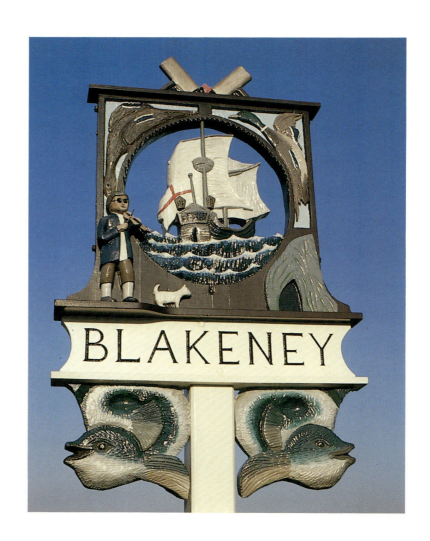

The village sign

Cley mill at dawn

Cley mill, with the R. Glaven and from across the marshes

Salthouse from the heath

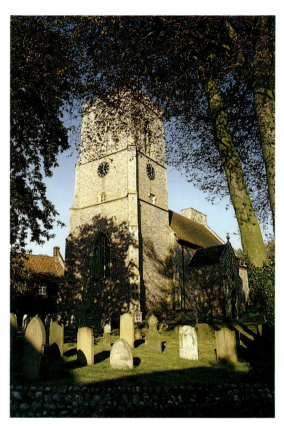

The churches at Salthouse and Weybourne (right)

Sunrise at Sheringham

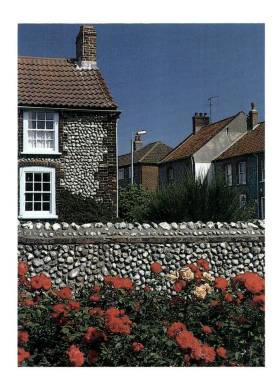

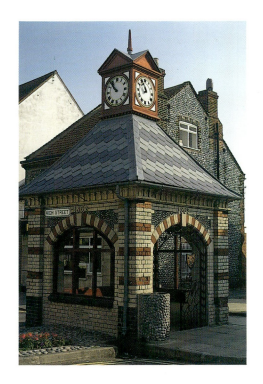

Beach flint at Sheringham
and two of its former uses

Sunset at East Runton

West Runton in winter

East Runton beach

Cromer Lifeboat:
Ruby and
Arthur Reed II

North east squall crossing Cromer Beach

Cromer pier at sunset

Cromer's east beach by moonlight

The Hotel de Paris at night

The pier in winter with repairs in progress

Welding work under the pier deck

The gangway and seafront buildings

Cromer church

Hauling crab-pots at sunrise

Paul Jeffries cooking crabs;
Brian Rogers and Willy Cox
lifting boat onto skeet;
John Jonas with part of his catch

Overstrand beach

Poppyland

Mundesley beach at sunrise

Stow Mill

Happisburgh church

Happisburgh lighthouse

Crab-boats returning home

Cover: *Cromer pier at sunrise*
Title: *After a gale at Mundesley*
Back: *Cromer lighthouse at dusk*
Photographs © Alan Blair 1989

Many of the photographs depicted here
are also available as postcards

Printed by:
Ancient House Press
Origination By:
Thetford Photolitho

First published in 1989
by ANGLIAN LANDSCAPES
Cromer, Norfolk
Tel: (0263) 514550